The Hard 90 Mindset
(Reach your full potential on the baseball field and in life.)

Eric Walczykowski

Contact author: ejw555@gmail.com

The purpose of this book is to educate parents on how to enhance
the performance of their developing baseball players. Nothing in
this book should be misconstrued as a medical diagnosis or
treatment or substitute for a diagnosis by a physician or qualified
healthcare provider. Should you have any healthcare-related
questions, please see your physician or healthcare provider before
starting a new treatment, diet, or fitness program. You should
never disregard medical advice or delay seeking it because of
something you read in this book.

The names of all players in this book have been changed to honor
their privacy.

This book is also available in e-book format.

Walczykowski, Eric.
The Hard 90 Mindset / by Eric Walczykowski

ISBN: 978-1-7347198-0-2

1.   Parenting - Sports 2. Parenting - Psychological Aspects 3.
Sports - Psychological

Printed in the United States of America.

Photo credits on the back cover to Jennifer Peatross Photography.

DEDICATION

To my three children, Taylor, Devon, and Jordan, who have been my partners in learning that improving our chances of fulfilling our dreams requires:

1. Spending the time needed to:
   - Write a detailed description of our dreams
   - Prepare a mission or set of accomplishments that are needed to reach our dreams
   - Develop a list of goals or steps to complete our mission
   - Plan our schedule to do the tasks to reach our goals

2. Embracing these core principles that guide our actions:
   - Do your best
   - Work as a team
   - Want it more
   - Always be open to learning and adapting

CONTENTS

SPECIAL THANKS

To my wife, Colleen Walczykowski, for being my copilot on life's journey and for her unwavering support of my passion for baseball as she endured the huge sacrifices required to move *Hard 90 Baseball* forward.

To my parents, Walt and Jan Walczykowski, for helping spark my passion for baseball and encouraging me to pursue my dreams with enthusiasm and commitment (and also for spending countless hours editing this book).

To Hard 90 general manager, Christy Sarabia, for believing in the Hard 90 mission and sharing her passion for baseball with the entire Hard 90 community.

To the Hard 90 Baseball family for supporting our mission and allowing us to be a small part of your athlete's baseball and life journey.

1 FOREWORD

In the spring of 2008, I had the opportunity to embark on a journey of coaching my oldest son, Devon, in the game of baseball. While I was ecstatic to give back to the game, I quickly realized that I was beginning an adventure that would bring me in contact with some amazing young men, families, and people in the baseball world.

Through this journey, I was adopted by several mentors who have had extremely successful careers in baseball, including:
—Dean Stotz (37-year associate head coach, Stanford University baseball team)
—Paul Cogan (special assistant, amatuer scouting, Los Angeles Dodgers)
—Tom Kunis (area scout, Los Angeles Dodgers, and college coach, Stanford University)
—Roc Murray (nearly four decades as a high school baseball coach)

Roc generously spent countless hours with me sharing concepts he and his family developed over decades of coaching the fundamentals of the game, utilizing the psychomotor (skills), cognitive (knowledge), and affective (attitude) domains of learning.

Through coaching, I quickly realized that baseball is about more than just the rules and mastery of the game; it affords young people an opportunity to learn valuable life lessons. Lessons that, if taught correctly and supported by the team (players, coaches, and family), could prepare them for success in their personal lives as well as in baseball.

Over the years, I have drawn upon my experience as an athlete, a student of martial arts, a father, a corporate executive, and the insights of others to develop a **MINDSET**— an established set of attitudes that incorporated both a core philosophy and systematic process to help players improve their chances of reaching their full potential.

"A ballplayer spends a good piece of his life gripping a baseball, and in the end it turns out that it was the other way around all the time."
—Jim Bouton

2 INTRODUCTION

It was the bottom of the 7th inning with two outs at the USA Baseball Regional Championships at the Big League Dreams Park in Manteca, CA. The Hard 90 14U team was down by two runs to a stacked Northern California All-Star team. Runners were on 1st and 2nd, and Bobby Thomas stepped up to the plate. The crowd was tense, but on the first pitch, Bobby hit the ball over the left field fence for a 3-run walk-off home run, and the fans went wild.

This was an exhilarating moment. A moment that many dream of—and yet there was Bobby, a confident, composed, 14U kid, seasoned with USA Baseball National Team experience.

It was no wonder that many believed he was going to hit that home run before it even happened. So why did Bobby exude so much confidence in that situation?

Why, at only 14, did Bobby already have USA National Team experience?

Why was Bobby an elite baseball player?

Why did Bobby make the other players on the team better?

Why did Bobby have a 4.0 GPA in school?

Why was Bobby a model son?

Why was Bobby the friend who every parent wanted their kid to have?

Was this just an accident that Bobby was able to thrive under pressure? Was Bobby born this way? Or did Bobby *learn* how to be this way?

I believe that competitive youth sports were a major factor that shaped Bobby mentally, emotionally, physically, socially, and intellectually for this situation. Specifically:

- The hours of training he put in from the time he was 8
- The coaches who helped mold him into a high-level athlete
- The supportive family that encouraged him

Youth sports provided the opportunity for Bobby to learn valuable life lessons that spilled over into every aspect of his life—as a son, friend, student, and athlete.

If Bobby could accomplish all of this through youth sports, I BELIEVE YOU CAN TOO!

So let's get started!

3 YOUTH SPORTS

"Play a sport. It will teach you how to win honorably, lose gracefully, respect authority, work with others, manage your time, and stay out of trouble."
—*Amanda Hohenberry*

Youth sports offer the greatest opportunity to shape the next generation of people. The training, discipline, skills, and competition provide young men and women with the opportunity to learn important principles, including:

- The value of hard work and quality effort
- The importance of a cohesive team
- The ability to overcome adversity and persevere
- The usefulness of learning from every situation—win or lose.

These principles, when internalized, become character traits that provide benefits well beyond the baseball diamond and serve many adults on a daily basis as guides to be productive and successful. In fact, many corporations seek applicants with elite athletic experience for their executive positions.

As a testament to the impact of youth sports on future generations, I would like to introduce Jacob Cha.

Jacob is set to attend Stanford University on a baseball scholarship. He started playing baseball at age 8 in a local recreation league. At the conclusion of the recreation league, he was selected to play on the all-star team before joining a travel baseball team. His father sought out the very best hitting coach to train him, and he began hitting three or four days a week in one-hour sessions. In addition, Jacob worked out with a strength-and-conditioning coach three days a week. This practice continued for the next several years as he played year-round travel baseball. In fact, by the age of 18, he had logged over 2,000 hours in private, one-on-one hitting instruction alone.

On the diamond, Jacob's skills were equivalent to elite varsity players in the area, and he started on the section-winning varsity baseball team all four years. In addition to baseball, Jacob played flag football and recreation basketball, earned straight A's in advanced, got a perfect SAT score, and maintained a girlfriend.

Behind all Jacob's success was a strong work ethic that included countless hours with tutors and private athletic coaches that taught him the value of hard work. In addition, his commitment and determination to do well was fueled by his dream of playing in the major leagues.

Many scoffed at the hours that Jacob invested honing his craft. Some said, "Jacob's dad is crazy," or Jacob was "robbed of his childhood." But I got to know Jacob's dad, and he was anything but crazy. He was a loving father and a great businessman. He knew the kind of effort it took to be successful and the work that was required to be a champion. His goal was simply to provide Jacob the opportunity to pursue his dream of playing professional baseball. But the blueprint and resources did more than that, as Jacob became a remarkable son and student as well.

As Jacob enters Stanford, he will be joining a unique tradition—a tradition called "rare air," the pinnacle of academics and athletics. Jacob will be in good company at Stanford: Its baseball players from 1980 to present day have gone on to do amazing things, including playing in the minor and major leagues and becoming captains of industry as doctors, lawyers, venture capitalists, and CEOs.

One thing that's clear is that after working directly with six Stanford baseball players over the years, Hard 90 has seen firsthand the effort that was put in to qualify for Stanford academically and athletically. Even clearer is that youth sports and the pursuit of excellence in youth sports molded the habits that turned into character traits that have fostered success both on the baseball field and in life.

"Winning is not a sometime thing, it is an all-the-time thing. You don't do things right once in a while. You do them right all the time. "
—*Vince Lombardi*

The Hard 90 Process

4 DREAM YOUR DREAM

"You can't put a limit on anything. The more you dream, the farther you get."
—*Michael Phelps*

Youth sports allow players to dream. In fact, dreaming is a huge part of being young and should be readily encouraged. Who's to say a player can't play Major League Baseball?

At Hard 90 Baseball, we encourage our players to DREAM BIG…

"if you shoot for the moon, you will end up among the stars."
—*Norman Vincent Peale*

…and learn some valuable lessons along the way.

"Impossible is just a big word thrown around by small men who find it easier to live in the world they've been given than to explore the power they have to change it. Impossible is not a fact. It's an opinion. Impossible is not a declaration. It's a dare. Impossible is potential. Impossible is temporary. Impossible is nothing."
—*Muhammad Ali*

When we encourage our kids to dream big, we are encouraging them to see what is possible in the world. These big dreams get our kids excited about the sport that serves as inspiration for them to put in the hard work that is required to become great. Passion is inspired through dreams.

The process of dreaming allows our kids to focus on positive things, filter out negativity, and enjoy a happier life. A great way to encourage kids to start the dreaming process is to ask them what they want to be when they grow up. Urge them to DREAM BIG— the bigger the dream, the more excitement and passion kids will have for making it happen.

In the movie "Field of Dreams," Terrance Mann highlighted the importance of dreaming and the role baseball has played in the "America of Dreams":

> *"The one constant through all the years, Ray, has been baseball. America has rolled by like an army of steamrollers. It's been erased like a blackboard, rebuilt, and erased again. But baseball has marked the time. This field, this game, is a part of our past, Ray. It reminds us of all that once was good, and that could be again. Oh, people will come, Ray. People will most definitely come."*

When a Hard 90 player says he wants to be a Major League Baseball player, we encourage him to describe a moment when he sees himself playing in a major league game. It is important for the player to describe this moment in as much detail as possible: describing what they see, what they hear, what they smell, and how they feel. This process of descriptive dreaming allows the player to make the dream as real as possible.

As Ronnie Lott eloquently stated:

> *"If you can believe it, the mind can achieve it."*

Again, we believe, thoughts are things; the more detailed the picture, the more real it becomes. The more real it becomes, the more passion our kids will have to pursue it. The more passion our kids have to pursue it, the more likely they will work hard and make their dreams a reality.

As part of this process, we also encourage our players to record their dreams on paper. Similar to using great details, writing down their dreams makes the dreams more real to the players. Recording their dreams also allows them to review them on a regular basis and keep them on the top of their minds.

On the next page, you will find an example of a template to record your dream.

DREAM

_____

_____

_____

_____

_____

_____

_____

_____

_____

_____

_____

_____

_____

_____

_____

"Baseball was, is, and always will be the greatest game in the world to me."
—Babe Ruth

One of our junior-high players at Hard 90 Baseball recorded this dream:

"It was a crisp day in the fall at Fenway Park. My Sox were taking on our rivals, the Yankees. In the locker room, the guys were gearing up for the last game of the season. It was bittersweet lacing up my spikes for the last time. I was slated to start that day in right field. I walked down the tunnel to the dugout. The announcer called my name, and I sprinted to right field to a thunderous ovation as I took my spot for my last game."

After recording your dream, put it somewhere you will see it and think about it often. The more you interact with your dream, the more real it will become, and you will be more apt to put in the work to make it a reality.

Finally, share your dream with family and friends. Through this process, you are enlisting team members to support you on your journey.

Don't be discouraged if people tell you it is not possible. Use that as fuel to make that dream happen.

"An athlete cannot run with money in his pockets. He must run with hope in his heart and dreams in his head." —*Emil Zatopek*

5 MISSION

"You have to expect things of yourself before you can do them."
—Michael Jordan

It is hard to stop a man on a mission.

A mission is a BIG thing you would like to accomplish a few years out. It is the next peak to shoot for on your way to climbing the mountain.

A mission is a guiding star that is closely aligned with your dream. While your dream may be 12 to 15 years away, your mission should be two to three years away.

Your mission will help you make daily decisions on how to spend your time.

Hard 90 Baseball is very active in helping players set their mission. In fact, one of our current junior-high players' mission is to make the varsity baseball team as a freshman. This player is in sixth grade and the mission of making the varsity team in ninth grade is three years away. His mission is directly in line with his dream of playing Major League Baseball and guides his weekly planning.

"Without self-discipline, success is impossible, period."
—Lou Holtz

When tough choices are to be made, this sixth-grader remembers his mission of making the varsity team as a freshman and uses it to guide his decision-making. Currently, he is training five days a week to accomplish his goal. And though daily he is asked by his friends to play video games after school, he chooses instead to do his homework to allow time for a quick meal and one of his three hourlong training sessions. Our Hard 90 player enjoys video games and plays them during the week, but he does not compromise his homework or practice to do so. His mission is displayed front and center on his bathroom mirror to remind him of his goal.

As with your dream, it is important to write down your mission and display it somewhere you will interact with it daily. Like our sixth-grade player, many of our other players display their mission on their bathroom mirror so they can review it while washing their hands or brushing their teeth each day.

Below, you will find a template to write down your mission:

MISSION

_____

_____

_____

_____

_____

_____

_____

_____

_____

_____

_____

_____

_____

_____

_____

"Make your life a mission — not an intermission."
—Arnold H. Glasgow

6 GOALS

*"There are only two options regarding commitment.
You're either IN or you're OUT. There is no such
thing as life in-between."*
—Pat Riley

Goal-setting is an integral part of reaching your mission and ultimately your dream. Think of your goals as a personal commitment to yourself.

As we discussed, a mission is two to three years out, and a goal should be six to 12 months out. A goal should be big and inspiring. A goal should be tied to your mission, which in turn is aligned with your dream.

Logic suggests that it is best to set **S.M.A.R.T.** goals for the **five fundamental tools of baseball.**

Specific: A specific area. For the athletes at Hard 90, they need to develop goals for each of the five fundamental tools of baseball (**hit, hit for power, run, field, and throw**).

Measurable: The goal must be something you can measure. For instance, a common **run** tool measurement for Hard 90 Baseball players is the 60-yard-dash time. A player might set a goal of reducing it to 6.8 seconds.

Attainable: The goal must be attainable within a period of time. A 13-year-old that throws the ball 75 mph might set a goal to throw 80 mph in nine months. This is something that—with hard work—could be attained. But setting a goal to throw 91 mph in nine months, it is highly unlikely that it will be attained, and in fact might discourage the athlete.

Relevant: The goal must be relevant **to the overall mission and dream.** This is why we use 5 Tool Athlete Goal Development at Hard 90 Baseball: Because these goals further a player's ability to excel in the game.

Time-bound: The goal must have a deadline. The timetable puts the urgency on the training necessary to accomplish the goal.

> *"Choosing a baseball goal and sticking to it changes everything."*
> *—Felicity Luckey*

Below is a goal template for you to use to set goals.

 # GOALS

_____

_____

_____

_____

_____

_____

_____

_____

"Set your goals high and don't stop until you get there."
—*Bo Jackson*

Once you have written down your goals, **review them against the S.M.A.R.T. criteria** to make sure that they are specific, measurable, attainable, relevant and have a time frame.

One of the Hard 90 eighth-grade players set the following goal in December:

"I want to hit the baseball 85 mph off a tee by September 1 of my first year of high school."

As you can see from the goal it is **specific**: hit the ball 85 MPH off a tee.

The goal is **measurable**: using a radar gun, you can track a ball's exit velocity.

This eighth-grader currently hits the ball 78 mph off a tee. Given he has nine months to attain 85 mph, Hard 90 believes that with the right work, he can **attain** this goal.

This eighth-grader's mission is to be an impact player on the JV team his freshman year. Therefore, hitting the ball 85 mph off of the tee is **relevant** to his mission.

The player would like to attain the goal by September 1, thus the goal is **time-based.**

Key: As a student-athlete, you should set both academic and athletic goals.

As with the dream and mission, put your goals in a place where you can review them daily. Our Hard 90 athletes use this condensed format:

MISSION

_____

_____

_____

_____

_____

_____

DREAM

_____

_____

_____

_____

_____

_____

GOALS

_____

_____

_____

_____

_____

_____

In addition to reviewing your goals daily, successful athletes share their goals with people who can help them achieve those goals. Some examples:

- Parents
- Family
- Teammates
- Coaches
- Trainers
- Teachers
- Scouts

By sharing your goals with others, you will start to **build a team of people** to strive and thrive with you on your journey.

7 WORK YOUR PLAN

Congratulations! You have now set the foundation to make your dream come true!

1. You have imagined a big **dream** in great detail and written it down to make it as real as possible.
2. You have written down a **mission**—a guiding light for you to make daily decisions, the first peak for you to ascend on the way to your dream.
3. You have written down specific **goals**—the first big steps to achieving your mission by providing you with a road map for planning your week.

"If you fail to plan, you are planning to fail."
—John Wooden

In order for you to achieve your goals, you need to plan out your time. Specifically, you need to **plan your athletic training, your academic studying and your social downtime.**

For your athletic training plan, there are generally two parts:

1. A well-thought-out plan for reaching your goals for each of the **five tools of baseball.** This should be a weekly plan to ensure that you are completing specific workouts designed to advance each of these tools.

- **Hit and Hit for Power:** The elite Hard 90 athletes train the "hit and hit for power tools" five to six days a week. The ideal training includes posture drills without a bat to create proper movement patterns, tee work, overhand front toss, and live hitting reps. The elite player also watches video of MLB players' swings and reads articles and books about hitting.

In addition to hitting, most elite athletes train their vision by learning to track types of pitches utilizing colored and numbered balls and by using phone apps.

- **Run:** At Hard 90, athletes practice a minimum of three to four days a week. The run tool training is usually incorporated in strength-and-conditioning training. It's been said that in order to run fast, you need to practice running fast. Good training includes form training and sprints at different intervals. Elite athletes always take the opportunity to improve their run tool by sprinting everywhere they go on the baseball field, including to and from their position each inning.

- **Field:** Generally, this is one of the most under-practiced. Field tool practice must be done two to three days a week. Simple ways to improve the field tool include throwing a lacrosse ball against a wall and throwing the ball in the air. Elite Hard 90 athletes train posture drills without a glove, fungo, and live game reps.

- **Throw:** The throw tool is one of the most debated topics in the game today. Some advocates believe that year-round throwing is the way to go, while others say that players need to take three to four months off per year. Elite Hard 90 players train the throw tool year-round, leveraging specific stretches, posture drills, bands, plyo balls, and long toss.

2. A plan for **strength and conditioning.** In general, players who aspire to play baseball at an elite level need strength-and-conditioning training three days a week under the supervision of a professional coach. From ages 8 to 13, strength and conditioning is mostly speed, agility, and body-weight movements; whereas for ages 14 and up, it incorporates weights. This program positively supports the five tools of baseball.

"The key is not the will to win. Everybody has that. It is the will to prepare to win that is important." — *Bobby Knight*

At Hard 90, we recommend planning a consistent time each week to accommodate both your **five tools** and **strength-and-conditioning** training workouts.

Below you will find a template for scheduling your athletic training plan.

WEEKLY ATHLETIC PLAN

GOAL	M	T	W	TH	F	SA	SU

In addition to a weekly athletic plan, it is important for athletes to develop a weekly academic plan as well. The following with help with that.

WEEKLY ACADEMIC PLAN

GOAL	M	T	W	TH	F	SA	SU

As part of any good training plan, it is necessary each week to **review the prior week's plan** - to look at <u>what was completed and how well</u> and <u>what was missed</u>. Specifically, it is important to consider how you executed each task and whether you went through these tasks considering their purpose and urgency. The pitfall that some athletes fall into is a "check the box" mentality: accomplishing tasks, but not putting in their best effort. This may lead to a "check mark," but could result in little or no real benefit.

All the information obtained from a review of a prior week's plan is critical for making adjustments or improvements to the following week's plan. Perhaps a helpful way to think about your plan is that each event you put on your sheet is <u>your commitment to yourself,</u> and fulfilling that commitment has the potential of bringing you another step closer to achieving your dream.

> *"Discipline is doing what has to be done, when it has to be done, as well as it can be done, and doing it that way all the time"* —Bobby Knight

The Hard 90 Philosophy

8 THE FOUR GUIDING PRINCIPLES

"Competitive sports are played mainly on a five-and-a-half inch court—the space between your ears." —Bobby Jones

Now that you have your dream, mission, goals, and weekly plans written down, it is time to get to work. The road to your dream will not be easy; just the sheer ability to stick to weekly planning alone will be difficult, let alone the setbacks you might encounter along the way through injuries, politics, and other things that might be deemed unfair.

You will encounter naysayers. You will at times question whether the pursuit of your dream is worth it. You will be given opportunities that seem great but really take you off track from accomplishing your goals.

This is why we developed the Hard 90 Philosophy, which is a set of underlying principles our coaches implement in their teaching. These principles allow athletes to filter every experience that comes their way and test its synergy and contribution to reaching the goal.

The 4 core principles to the Hard 90 Philosophy are:

1. Do your best
2. Work as a team
3. Want it more
4. Always learn

While these may be simple words and you might not understand their meaning or context, stick with us and we will unlock how these four simple principles can help you as you travel toward achieving your dream.

"You can motivate by fear, and you can motivate by reward. But both those methods are only temporary. The only lasting thing is self-motivation." —Homer Rice

9 DO YOUR BEST

"The highest compliment that you can pay me is to say that I work hard every day, that I never dog it." — *Wayne Gretzky*

When you wake up each morning, you have the opportunity to make that day your very best day ever. This mentality takes into account that time is a blessing, and in order for you to honor the blessing, you need to use it wisely, effectively, and for something worthwhile. This is not to say that each day will be perfect. But successful people give their best effort daily, because they know that success is based on a cumulation of best efforts focused on their dream.

"Make each day your masterpiece."
—John Wooden

Life is a journey, not a destination—a marathon, not a sprint. Yet sometimes when we are in the daily grind, it feels like we are losing.

At these times, it is important to realize that in the process of achieving your goals, it is critical that you always commit your best effort. Some days you will be 4-for-4, some you will be 0-for-4. The important thing is that by giving your all you are making progress, because even if you fail, it may just provide information for an adjustment that could lead to success in the future.

Doing your best is a combination of focus and grit. This is not just a sports-focused mentality, it translates to all aspects of your life. You need to do your best at being a son/daughter, friend, teammate, student, and athlete.

"Today, you have 100 percent of your life left."
—*Tom Landry*

Do you make your bed when you get up in the morning? What does making your bed have to do with doing your best? This is a simple way to start your day off as a champion. You wake up and you complete a task that is totally in your control.

Are you early or late for school or class? Champions are early, champions are prepared. If you are consistently late for class, you create more friction, which in turn creates more stress, preventing you from doing your best.

Do you do the minimum—only what is required—getting things done just before the deadline? Or do you take every opportunity you are given and put in the maximum effort?

Winning is a habit. Unfortunately, so is losing. — *Vince Lombardi*

The more you practice giving your best effort to each task, the more natural it becomes. The more natural it becomes, the more successful you will become in everything you pursue.

Tony Dansic attended a very successful Pac-12 school as a pitcher. Tony had unbelievable success at this school, winning first-team all-conference honors three times. While many might be surprised by Tony's success, Hard 90 was not surprised at all. Tony was the first to arrive and the last to leave practices and games.. Tony studied all aspects of the game and developed his personal baseball routine to allow him to be a successful D1 pitcher.

Tony was internally driven and gave his best effort to every task. The first thing he did every morning was make his bed. When he received a homework assignment, he did it immediately. This mentality allowed him to earn grades in the top one percent of his class.

Tony proved that practicing and making a habit of applying your best effort to every task increases the possibility of having success in all aspects of life.

"Plan your work and work your plan." —*Marv Levy*

Players who subscribe to the Hard 90 philosophy and process "plan their work and work their plan." This allows them to put maximum effort into the tasks in front of them.

When you are at home, do you see a need and fill it? When you walk by the trash and it needs to be taken out, do you take it out without being asked?

When you are done with your dish, do you leave it at the table for someone else to clear, or do you rinse it and put it in the dishwasher?

Dean Stotz, a 37-year associate head coach at Stanford University, tells a famous story about leaving a Styrofoam cup on the baseball field and watching to see which prospective recruits picked up the cup. To Dean, the players who picked up the cup showed positive character attributes that were consistent with players he wanted at Stanford.

At Hard 90 we believe the following are key attributes for doing your best:

- ☐ Developing a dream, a mission, and goals
- ☐ Planning your time
- ☐ Being on time
- ☐ Being prepared
- ☐ Focusing on the task you are currently working on
- ☐ Giving maximum effort to what you are currently working on
- ☐ Evaluating your performance honestly
- ☐ Making adjustments to achieve great success
- ☐ Evaluating your daily, weekly, and monthly actions toward the achievement of your goals

"Most people never run far enough on their first wind to find out they've got a second." —*William James*

The hard fact about success is most people do not achieve their dreams because of a lack of effort—they give up too soon.

- • They fail to understand that success takes time, but if you commit

to do your best over a
sustained period, it will produce results.

- They fail to understand that a temporary setback could be just that—temporary—and
they miss the lesson and insight into how to do things differently.

- They define their best effort in relation to people around them and therefore define their competition too narrowly.

The truth is that in order for you to make it, you need to be better than the people you know and the people you do not know. If you are trying to make it in baseball, your competition is the entire world. There are impoverished countries that you are competing against that see baseball as a way to eat—are you working at it like your life depends on it?

At Hard 90, we had a player who played on our C team. Not the A team, not the B team, but the C team. This player once broke his nose catching pop-ups before a game.

This player did not change organizations because he was on the C team. This players' parents did not use politics, money, or influence to get him on the A team. This player committed to the process—the grind and the training—and now he pitches for Stanford University. Whether or not he ever pitches in the big leagues, he will get a four-year degree from one of the top-five universities in the nation, because he committed to the process.

NOTE TO PARENTS: Do not make the road easier for your player. Commit to the process. If you want your player to succeed, allow them to struggle through the process with grit and determination, doing their best every day.

10 WORK WITH YOUR TEAM

"Teamwork is the secret that makes common people achieve uncommon results." —*Ifeanyi Onuoha*

In life, not one of us can claim full responsibility for our success. Even the most independent people had a mom that gave birth to them, and most people had someone raise them in their formative years, providing at a minimum food and shelter.

At Hard 90, we teach our players to value and respect their team. Teams will help you reach your goals. Teams will pick you up when you fail or when you are not feeling the ability to give your best. Teams will challenge you to strive beyond what you think is possible.

If you have a big dream, your team (coaches and fellow players) are extremely important. You need to seek out coaches and mentors who have the knowledge and the desire to help you get where you want to go. In baseball, you can tell if people have these qualities by their track record of helping other players go on to play high school, college, and professional baseball. At Hard 90, we are fortunate to have over 350 players who have played in the collegiate and professional ranks.

The right coach or mentor on your team will not only teach you the fundamentals you need to learn to be successful, but they will help you learn values and habits that sustain you in your journey and beyond.

For this reason, teamwork (with coaches and fellow players) is one of the core values we emphasize at Hard 90. This value is critical, because we have seen that players have a higher probability of reaching their dreams if they work with others who are like-minded. With all else being equal, coaches, in general, will give more opportunities in high school, college, and the pros if the player is a team player.

Ron Smith was a standout travel and high school baseball player. His performance earned him an opportunity to play on a Pac-12 program as a catcher. However, due to competition, he lost his spot and bounced back to junior college where he could play more. From junior college, he was drafted by the Milwaukee Brewers. He spent five years in the Brewers organization with a strong glove and a marginal bat, because he was a team guy. As a catcher, he knew that his role was to help develop new pitchers, not be the star. As a result, the Brewers organization always looked for opportunities to help him continue his dream of playing professional baseball.

The Lesson: in addition to finding the right coaches, supporting your teammates is important. The road to a big dream is long and filled with tough challenges and sacrifices. Working as a team player has its benefits, because providing mutual support can not only make baseball more fun, it can help lead you right into the dream of your choice!

"The main ingredient of stardom is the rest of the team." —John Wooden

At Hard 90, one of the ways we teach teamwork is to share information about opposing pitchers and umpires. Our players are taught from a very young age to communicate information about pitchers and umpires in the dugout after at-bats. This invaluable information gives our hitters a leg up when they step into the box.

For instance, one of the players on our elite junior-high team (full of Pac-12 commits) had picked up a "tell"on an opposing pitcher when he was going to throw his changeup. This player shared this tell with all of his teammates, making them more successful at the plate. We beat this pitcher continuously during that season (while others teams struggled), as our hitters knew when they were going to get a fastball. Against great pitching, it is much easier to hit when you know which pitch is coming.

In addition to helping you succeed, teammates are a great group to wage friendly competition—who can throw the hardest, hit the farthest, or run the fastest. Over the years, Hard 90 teams compete with their teammates in a friendly manner. This spirit of competition has led players to ratchet up their efforts to accomplish their dreams on the baseball field.

Felix Garcia, a former Hard 90 player and current professional ball player, said, "I was never going to let my teammates get a leg up by outworking me. If they were going to train, I was going to train harder."

This type of competitive camaraderie encourages players to challenge themselves to do great things and make mature, calculated choices.

Another former Hard 90 player said, "I spent my Friday nights in high school at the clubhouse training and having fun in baseball. It was easy to stay out of trouble, because all of my friends were training with me at the clubhouse."

As you can see, being part of a team is clearly a huge advantage on your road to accomplishing your dream. Teams help you make the right choices, push you to be the best you can be, pick you up when you are not doing well, give you a leg up on the competition, and give you the right information you need to become all you can be. Be good to your team!

"No individual can win a game by himself." —Pele

11 WANT IT MORE

"Obstacles don't have to stop you. If you run into a wall, don't turn around and give up. Figure out how to climb it, go through it, or work around it."
—Michael Jordan

Your journey to your dream will be filled with obstacles. People, politics, injuries, and many other things may get in your way. Your success will not be determined by what gets in your way, but how you react to it.

You need to want it more. You need to want it more than your circumstances should allow you to want it. You need to want it more than the people around you. You need to want it so much that you will take your circumstance, deal with it head on, and find a way around it, through it, over it, under it, or whatever it takes to keep moving forward.

There are many natural events in baseball that seem unfair that allow you to practice "wanting it more" on a daily basis.

Take the umpire, for example. Go to any baseball field on any given day, and you will hear people complaining about the umpire. That pitch was high, that pitch was outside, he missed the tag—the complaining goes on. You hear it from the players, coaches, parents, and fans.

The cold, hard facts are that complaining is merely an excuse. <u>It is easier to make an excuse than to accept the reality that you did not make an adjustment.</u>

"Excuses are for people that don't want it bad enough." —*Ken Lear*

Winners find a way to deal with their circumstances. Winners find a way to use whatever is deemed unfair to their advantage.

At Hard 90, we teach our players to assess the situation and formulate a plan to succeed in spite of the circumstances. For instance, if the umpire is calling pitches outside, our hitters are instructed to move closer to the plate and look to drive the ball the opposite way.

In the same circumstance, we teach our catchers to test the umpire's zone in the first inning. If we can establish a pitch away off the plate for a strike, we will use that to our advantage all day.

Instead of making excuses, we find a way! These small practices add up and eventually you start looking at mishaps as an opportunity. You will not dwell on the problem, but immediately you will jump to potential solutions.

"Most people give up just when they're about to achieve success. They quit on the one-yard line. They give up at the last minute of the game one foot from a winning touchdown." —*Ross Perot*

Baseball offers great opportunities to practice **resilience** when it comes to playing time. In today's instant-gratification society, players and parents demand playing time at choice spots, regardless of whether they are the best player or not.

Many times players will say that the coach is unfair or likes another player better. Do you hear the excuse?

At Hard 90, we teach our players that if they want to ensure their playing time, they need to be demonstrably better than anyone else on the team. This means to make it really clear who the best player is by working harder than anyone else. If you are not demonstrably better than anyone else on your team, how can you hope to accomplish your dream of playing high school, college, or professional baseball? As you move up the ranks, your competition goes from your team, to your city, to your country, and eventually to the whole world.

Use the lack of playing time as fuel to work harder. Take the initiative to ask the coach which areas of your game you need to improve to earn more playing time.

The great basketball coach John Wooden said that one of his greatest motivation tactics was "the bench." Players who did not give their best effort ended up on the bench, so they could reflect on their lack of effort.

> *"Adversity causes some men to break; others to break records." —William A. Ward*

John Clingsmith, one of our players at Hard 90 Baseball, was at a big out-of-town tournament. This particular tournament was on the other side of the country, and his family spent thousands of dollars for him to be able to play in it. John struggled with morning games. At this particular tournament, the team had to play one evening until midnight and then turn around the next morning and play at 8:00 a.m.

In the morning game, John took the field in the first inning and made an error that cost the team two runs. Errors in baseball happen, and errors where 100-percent effort is given are not a problem. But on this particular error, John did not give 100 percent and he was benched after the first inning. John was the best player at his position but had let the team down, because he did not prepare himself to play.

After the fourth inning, John went up to the coach declaring that he was ready to play. The coach left him on the bench for the rest of the game, and this particular benching precluded John from getting equal playing time with the rest of the team.

In the next game John came out ready to play with more effort than he had ever given. In fact, he worked with his parents to design a routine to wake up in the morning and be ready for morning games. Never again did John make an error in morning games due to a lack of effort.

Instead of making an excuse, John and his family took this circumstance when he was 12 years old and dealt with it head-on. This allowed John to grow as a player and receive honors in his high school and college baseball career.

The Lesson: when it comes down to it, are you going to make an excuse or rise to the occasion and deal with your misfortune head on? Winners will take the challenge and find a way.

12 ALWAYS LEARN

"You win when you lose, if you learn." —*Richard Lee*

You can turn any loss into a win by learning something. Baseball is a game of failure; even the very best players fail more than they succeed.

If you learn something every time you fail, you will become a better player. This mindset will also allow you to play with less stress and truly enjoy the game. The most successful players know that the worst possible thing that could happen to them on the diamond is that they will get better from negative experiences. This allows them to focus on doing their very best in each situation.

Several years ago, our Hard 90 player Wyatt Pitowski consistently had trouble swinging the bat in big situations. Wyatt would freeze up when the pressure was intense and strike out time after time. But Wyatt's Hard 90 team was not going to let this be Wyatt's end. The coaches instead constantly reminded Wyatt that each time he was in one of those high-pressure situations, he was getting better for the next one. Through this experience, Wyatt learned that baseball is a process sport, and baseball rewards the process.

Wyatt was able to learn that a pressure at-bat is really no different than any other at-bat. Wyatt was in control of his mindset, and if he went to the plate expecting to swing, good things would happen. Over the course of the season, Wyatt took more swings in pressure situations. The process was rewarded and Wyatt learned a lot working through the process. Wyatt went on to be a clutch hitter in high school, all because he learned from his mistakes.

"The principle is competing against yourself. It's about self-improvement, about being better than you were the day before." —*Steve Young*

The Lesson: your success will be directly affected by how you deal with failure. Emotion can prevent you from dealing with failure in a productive way.

Hard 90 has seen over the years that many young players get very frustrated after a strikeout, an error, or other failure on the field. This frustration can manifest in everything from tears to shutting down from anger and throwing equipment.

For optimal success, it is very important to understand that failure is part of the game.

As Babe Ruth eloquently stated:

"Every strike brings me closer to my next home run."

While many have read this quote, few truly internalize the simple essence of what the Great Babe was saying:

Every strike— every strike that I took, swung and missed, or hit foul—every failure gives me knowledge that I can use to have success on the next pitch.

At Hard 90, we say the most important pitch is the next pitch. To truly focus on the next pitch, we help our players establish a routine to deal with failure, learn from it, and focus all of their attention on the next pitch.

"What do you do with a mistake: recognize it, admit it, learn from it, forget it." —*Dean Smith*

If an infielder makes an error, we teach him to take a deep breath, tell himself that he is going to get the ball on the next pitch, and then tell the pitcher to get him another ground ball. This routine is practiced, allowing for greater success in the game.

In addition to helping players understand that failure is part of the game, we want them to know that great teams build a culture to deal with failure that starts with the player, extends to teammates, is modeled by the coaching staff, and supported by the families.

This culture reinforces that failure is part of the game. The culture learns from failure and supports all of the energy being placed on the next pitch.

One of the ways we implement this at Hard 90 is that when a player strikes out, he takes the information from the at-bat and shares it with the on-deck batter and the rest of the bench. This allows the player to process his at-bat, and by sharing the knowledge he directs the rest of the team to focus on the next pitch.

This strong culture that supports learning from failure helps create the invincible athlete that does not play the game timidly. He plays it with joy, expecting good things to happen.

"I've learned that something constructive comes from every defeat." —Tom Landry

13 SUMMARY

The value of hard work and quality effort

The importance of a team

The ability to overcome adversity and persevere

The usefulness of learning from every situation

The passion to dedicate time to the dream

For every dream, there is always a backstory—a personal experience that gets in your blood and compels you to have passion. It is from my personal backstory that I had my start that propelled me through my journey and eventually an understanding of what I call the Hard 90 Mindset.

As a boy, I was "adopted" by my O-pa (grandfather in German) as a second son. Mind you, I had a dad and mom and sister, but my O-pa loved me deeply and wanted every opportunity to spend time with me and share his passion for baseball.

In the early years, I would spend hours and hours listening to his stories about his baseball heroes—Babe Ruth, Lou Gehrig, Ty Cobb—and the details of games he listened to on the radio as a kid. Baseball during the Depression and World War II (when my O-pa was young) was a saving grace As one president perceptively said, "Baseball is important to national morale." My O-pa knew about all the Hall of Famers and made sure I did, too. It was in my blood, and I would spend countless hours in my backyard throwing the ball up in the air and recounting games as I caught the ball and tagged players out. And each time the announcer flashed my name on the big screen, and the crowd broke out in a roar.

As I grew older, my O-pa would get out the newspaper every time I came and we would pore over baseball statistics like the batting averages of greats Willie McCovey, Mike Schmidt, Pete Rose, as well as newcomers Andre Dawson, Ryne Sandberg, Rickey Henderson, and Will Clark. He told me stories about a young baseball player who he taught in high school, Keith Hernandez, and how Keith was never without his precious baseball cards. My O-pa eventually took me to one of Keith's games so I could meet him and get his autograph on the cover of Sports Illustrated.

My grandfather loved baseball, and as I started to play in Little League and beyond, he was my biggest fan, driving 30 miles to watch and cheer my games. He coached me about what to look out for and how to improve. I worked hard on my stats so I could share with him my successes.

And then one day, he moved out of state and didn't come back.

To put it mildly, I was crushed. But slowly, I refocused and relied on other people who loved the game as well—especially my teammates on the field—many of whom are still my friends three-plus decades later. Baseball had gotten in my blood, and I doubled down to pique the interest of college recruiters in high school. After a short stint at Fresno State in the early 90s, I was done with baseball, but baseball was not done with me.

For years, I turned my attention to my career and family, only to have baseball—once again—secure a place in my life when I began to coach my two sons before eventually buying the Hard 90 Baseball School.

Over time, I have listened, participated, persevered, adjusted, studied, coached, and dedicated time to sifting through the details to glean the essence of baseball. My goal was no longer to play, but to share in the legacy. For from the field comes valuable life lessons for those who pick up their bats and gloves.

Dreams take you places. It is when you unite mind, body, and soul to reach your full potential in them that you achieve things that make them a reality. And you will ultimately learn that what you were really dreaming all along was to accomplish something significant.

As I've written, who is to say you can't play Major League Baseball?

DREAM YOUR DREAM

ABOUT HARD 90 BASEBALL

Hard 90 Baseball is a training facility in El Dorado Hills, California. Hard 90 offers classes and private lessons for hitting, pitching, and fielding. In addition to training, Hard 90 fields travel baseball teams for ages 9 to 18. Since its establishment in 2005, over 300 Hard 90 alumni have gone on to play college and professional baseball. www.hard90baseball.com

ABOUT THE AUTHOR

Eric Walczykowski is a husband, father, baseball coach and corporate executive. Through the years, Eric has had the opportunity to serve technology and life science companies as CEO, Division President, Venture Capitalist, Board Member and Advisor.

Since 2014, Eric and his wife Colleen have owned Hard 90 Baseball in El Dorado Hills, CA. Eric is a strong believer that sports is one of the greatest opportunities to teach youth about life.

Made in the USA
Las Vegas, NV
21 May 2021